BENT

BUT NOT

BROKEN

JACQULINE DAWSON

PAGE PUBLISHING, INC.
New York, NY

First originally published by Page Publishing, Inc. 2019

ISBN 978-1-64424-349-7 (Paperback)
ISBN 978-1-64424-350-3 (Digital)

Printed in the United States of America

ACKNOWLEDGMENTS

First off, I would like to thank God for his guidance, wisdom, and love. Also, I would like to thank my mom, my family, and my friend Valerie Banks-Jones for all their support, especially my children, who are my biggest supporters and promoters. A very special thanks to my grandson who illustrated and to my daughter Jalisa Dawson-Muniz for her long hours and dedication to my project, editing and reading, and for her computer skills. I couldn't have done it without you. I truly thank you.

PREFACE

In 1995–2007, I was in love with the man of my dreams, my best friend, my lover, and my protector. We had twelve beautiful years together, and in an instant, that all change after the death of my love. I became broken, depressed, and isolated from the world. I took my daughter and went to the mountains, where I could find myself again. In that time, I decided that God and my daughter Jalisa were my biggest encouragers. God led me to understand that although I was bent, I was not ever broken. Through prayer, he allowed me to open my door to other women and share our trials with each other. God shined his light, helping us to see and giving us the strength to do something together that I couldn't do alone, and just like that, Women of Encouragement was started. My desire is that my revealing my own truth will inspire you to share yours. We all struggle in our own ways. I always say, "Where there is struggle, there is strength."

INTRODUCTION

I'd like to introduce you to the characters of the book *Bent but Not Broken*. There are three main characters. Their names are Kelly, Kim, and Vanessa. This book speaks to obedience, disobedience, prayer, and restoration. How God strategically moves in our lives through events and situations that would and could destroy us. How disobedience can cause friction in the move of God in our lives. It speaks of prayer and restoration. How prayer changes things and restores us to wholeness in God. How obedience keeps straight the path that God has for us. These three women live different lives. They come together in God and grace, bringing in other women.

Vanessa starts her own women's group called Women of Encouragement through the word and the love of God. She empowers them to walk in a way pleasing to God, showing them how God moves on our behalf, continually protecting us from all harm and danger.

Kim, who is not a believer, lives a wayward life. However, intercessory prayer changed her life when Kelly and Vanessa prayed on her behalf. God restored them, bringing their life into alignment, showing us how the sick are healed, the blind see, and the lame walk. These women together encourage each other through God's leading and love.

PRAYER

I pray this book will reach many people at a wide range in hopes of helping them to love and embrace who God created them to be. The willingness to intercede on the behalf of others and their families in the words "it takes a village to raise a community" kind of way. Meaning, God is the head, and we follow him by helping others. Love means to encourage and empower others to move in God, greet one another in love, and showing in love and compassion for one another. I believe this is the greatest gift of all.

I pray this book will encourage and restore families, as well as heal the downtrodden. God says that he has sent the Word and healed the sick. I pray this book will touch and heal someone's soul and bring us closer as a people. I ask you to read this book and enjoy it then pass it along to others so that it may reach generations to come. I pray that God keeps and blesses you all. May this book encourage all that reads it in the spirit, for it was written in love. This is Jacquline saying peace and love.

THE JOURNEY BEGAN

Vanessa was living in a small town called Surehill with her mother, whom she took care of. They attended church regularly. She loved to be of service to others. Her mom had been diagnosed with cancer, and her dad was murdered a few months ago. Vanessa hadn't had time to grieve over her father's death. When her mother died, now all she had was her dreams of becoming a lawyer in the big city of New York. The Big Apple. However, she hadn't forgotten her mother's views of the big city life. Her mom would say, "The city is where the sin is, and if not careful, it would swallow a person whole."

Vanessa didn't have many friends, but she had her best friend, Kelly, who once lived in Surehill. Kelly decided to move out to the big city. Kelly always called Vanessa, trying to get her to come out there to live, but Vanessa never did consider until now. Now that her mom had passed on, Kelly would be in Surehill for the home-going of Vanessa's mom.

Kelly gave Vanessa a one-way plane ticket to come and stay with her, and after some time, Vanessa was beginning to think what it would be like living in the city. After her mom's death, she was spending all her time alone. And now she was feeling the loneliness of her mom's being gone. Now she began to think to herself, she had nothing left in Surehill to keep her there. She thought about her dream and felt God nudging her to take a chance and head on to New York.

Vanessa had been walking past this plane ticket long enough. She picked it up and thought to herself, *This doesn't have to be the end. Maybe this is just the beginning.* She smiled and began to thank God for the opportunity. She packed her things and headed to the airport on her way to New York. On the plane, Vanessa was having a lot of mixed emotion. She was sad for leaving her hometown and frightened of the unknown. She was even excited about the new life that awaits her.

VANESSA ARRIVAL

When the plane landed in New York, waiting for her was Kelly and Kim. Vanessa was so happy to see Kelly, whom she hadn't seen for what seemed like forever. They embraced each other. Kelly was standing beside a beautiful dark-skinned woman. She was short and thin. Kelly introduced her as Kim, and they also embraced each other. They pulled up to Kelly's house. Kim hadn't said a word the whole ride; she was there texting on her phone. They got out of the car, standing before her lovely white house. Two children and a nice-looking brown-skinned man stood smiling in front of the house.

Kelly introduced them as her children, Fey and Jimmy, and her husband, Dan. They all went into the house. Vanessa complimented how lovely Kelly's house was. Kelly thanked her and said, "Let me show you to your room."

She took Vanessa up to a lovely big bedroom upstairs and told her to make herself at home. Vanessa unpacked and went and took a shower. Kim decided to go home, and Kelly went back downstairs and got freshened up and started to prepare for dinner. As they sat down to eat, Vanessa was pleased to have a home-cooked meal. Vanessa complimented Kelly on dinner, and Kelly said, "Thank you."

Dan made a joke, saying she usually burned the house down, and they all laughed. When dinner was over, the kids washed and got ready for bed. Dan and Kelly and Vanessa sat down and had a drink. Dan and Kelly assured Vanessa she could stay there until she found an apartment. Kelly, being a realtor, would help her find something suitable and affordable. Kim had told Vanessa her job was looking for help in a law firm and set her up an appointment.

The following day, the women would meet for lunch at a little coffee shop that Kelly and Kim frequently went. They sat down and ordered water and coffee until they figure out what they were going to eat. They began talking.

Kim seemed to have an attitude. She was not talking much but on her phone, texting crazy. Kelly asked, "What's going on with you, Kim?"

Kim was snappy and said, "I thought you wanted to spend your time talking to Miss Country Time here."

Vanessa was angry now and said, "I don't care what's wrong with her. I didn't come for her, so she better stop coming for me. This country girl will give you a hell of an ass whooping."

Kim and Vanessa went back and forth, arguing, and Kelly yelled to them to stop. So they continued lunch, saying nothing to each other for a minute. Then Kelly announced to Vanessa that she found an apartment for her, and she gave her the keys. She said, "We can go today if you would like to see it."

Vanessa was very excited. She continually thanked Kelly. Kim rolled her eyes and said she had to go to meet Mike and she would talk to them later. Then she walked away. Kelly and Vanessa went to look at the apartment, and it was a few houses from Kelly. They walked in, and Vanessa loved it. Vanessa said, "It's lovely. It's furnished, and it's near. I love it. Thank you. Now I have to get some new clothes for this job so I can look the part." They both laugh.

VANESSA NEW APARTMENT

Vanessa moved in that night. The next day was the shopping day. The girls got together to shop for clothes for Vanessa's new job. They were having a great time laughing and trying on new clothes and shoes and things. They sat in the coffee shop, drinking coffee and laughing. Kelly invited them over for dinner. Later that evening, they all got together at Kelly's house and enjoyed great food and drinks and music. Kim came over to Vanessa and said, "I'm sorry about the other day."

Vanessa looked at Kim, and they began to laugh. Kim started to talk with Vanessa and told her of the affair she was having with Mike, a married man. Vanessa didn't understand how Kim, a beautiful woman who could have any man she wanted, would lower her standards to want to be with someone married. Why not get someone who loves you and just you? By looking at her, you can tell she can have any man she wants.

Kim shook her head and said, "I love him, and it's complicated."

Kelly walked in the room. "What's up, ladies?"

"Nothing, we were just talkin'," said Kim.

"That's good," said Kelly, and she gave them a group hug. "So how's the apartment," asked Kelly to Vanessa.

"It's lovely. I only wish my mom could be here to see it all," said Vanessa.

They all looked at each other and gave Vanessa a hug. They said, "We know you miss your mom."

Vanessa decided it was time for her to say goodnight. She had to get ready for her big day at the new job. Then Kim said she was going to be leaving as well for work, too, so they said good night.

VANESSA BIG DAY

Vanessa's first day at work, she headed into the office. As she walked down the hall, she realized all eyes were on her. She was getting all kinds of unwelcoming stairs and hearing all the whispering voices. Vanessa wondered why all eyes were on her. She continued to walk toward the boss's office and ran right into the boss, Mr. Davis. He looked up and said, "Hello, I'm Mr. Davis. Welcome. Let me show you your office."

As they walked down the hall, they ran into Kim. They said hello as if they didn't know each other. Mr. Davis put some folders on the desk. Then instructed Vanessa on what she was to do with them. He asked if she could handle this.

"Yes," said Vanessa.

"Then I'll leave you to it," said Mr. Davis, and he walked out.

Vanessa began to work on the folders. Kim appeared at the door and said, "Hey, we are meeting for drinks later at Kelly's house."

"Okay," said Vanessa.

"Enjoy," said Kim.

Vanessa continued to work on the folders on her desk. She thought to herself, *Thank God for the peaceful sleep I got last night in my new apartment.*

The day was going smooth, except for the whispering and staring. Vanessa didn't care much because in her mind she wasn't there to make friends, just there working to pay the rent. At the end of the day, Vanessa waited at the elevator for Kim, who was her ride to work and home. Kim arrived with her big mouth yelling, "Hey, boo! How was your day?"

Entering the elevator, Vanessa said, "Except for the nasty looks and whispering, it was a good day."

They were other way to to Kelly's house. They pulled up to the house for dinner. During the conversation at the table, Kelly asked Kim how it was going with Mike.

Kim said, "I haven't talked with Mike in a few days now." Two hours later, Kim's phone started blowing up. "It's Mike."

They pleaded with Kim not to answer it, but she did minutes later. She was out the door, heading to Mike's for a booty call.

"See y'all," said Kim, and she walked out the door. Shortly after, Vanessa finished her drink and headed home, which was a few houses down from Kelly.

"Good night, all," said Vanessa, hugging Kelly, and she walked out. Vanessa walked into the house; she could feel the emptiness. She missed her mom being there to welcome her home and talk to her. Vanessa walked into the dining room and picked up her mom's picture and shed a few tears. Then she went upstairs, took a shower, and went to bed. The next day at work, Vanessa and Kim made their way to work. They went their separate ways.

Vanessa reached her office and found more folders on her desk. She made a cup of coffee and began to work. Vanessa called Kelly.

"Hey, how's it going?" said Vanessa.

"Okay, I guess," said Kelly, but from the sound of her voice, something was wrong.

"Are you sure?" asked Vanessa.

"I'm okay," said Kelly. "I will talk to you later." And they hung up. Vanessa went back to work.

Later that day, Mr. Davis asked Vanessa if she would mind doing some overtime on a case he was working on. Vanessa said she didn't mind, But it was the way he was looking at her. He looked so strange. Mr. Davis walked out.

Vanessa got ready to meet Kim for lunch. Vanessa told Kim she was worried about Kelly, and she asked if she had spoken with Kelly.

"No," said Kim, "but we can stop over after work and check on her."

"Okay."

It was something in her voice that worried Vanessa. They stopped by Kelly's house and rang the bell and continued knocking and calling for Kelly. They got no response. They tried calling on the phone, no answer.

"She must be outside," said Kim. They left. Vanessa decided she would continue trying to contact Kelly but still no response.

It was late that night, while Vanessa lay in bed, when the doorbell rang. It was Kelly standing in the doorway. Vanessa pulled her inside and closed the door.

"Where have you been? We were looking for you. Where have you been?" asked Vanessa.

"My mother's house," said Kelly. "I left the kids there." Kelly looked a mess.

"So what's going on?" asked Vanessa.

"He is cheating on me," said Kelly.

Vanessa told Kelly to stay over her house, and she called Kim. They all got together and stayed over Vanessa's house, consoling Kelly.

The next day, Kim went home. Vanessa got herself together for work. Kelly was still asleep while Vanessa was making coffee. Kelly walked into the kitchen.

"Good morning. How are you feeling?" said Vanessa.

"Okay, I guess," said Kelly. She said she was going home to take a shower. Vanessa said she would call when she got to work, and she walked out the door. Kim pulled up outside, and she and Vanessa headed to work. The morning was going well until lunchtime. At lunch, Vanessa noticed Kim not talking much but texting angrily on her phone; and by her facial expression, she wasn't feeling what was being texted back to her. Vanessa, thinking it was Mike, told Kim to hang up on his dumb ass, but Kim nodded and smiled at her and continued texting. Just then, the phone rang, and she answered it, walking away from the table, yelling at the person on the other end of the phone.

Vanessa, still thinking it was Mike, got up, emptied her tray, and walked past Kim. She said she was going back to work. Kim waved her off and continued yelling into the phone. Vanessa didn't see Kim the rest of the day until it was time to go home. On the way home, Vanessa asked Kim about the phone call. Kim hesitated and then said she could handle it. Vanessa could tell Kim wasn't in the mood to talk about it, so she changed the subject and asked if Kim spoke to Kelly today.

"No," said Kim. "We can stop by and check on her."

Pulling up to Kelly's house, they noticed Kelly's car parked, but Dan's car wasn't there. They walked up to Kelly's door and rang the bell. Kelly answered and opened the door, wearing sweats and a tee, her hair up in a ponytail and her hazel eyes red from crying. Kelly was a beautiful woman, and it was hard seeing her like this, looking a mess. So to their surprise, Kelly opened the door. Both Kim's and Vanessa's mouths dropped wide open. They walked in, noticing the couch had covers on it, as if she had been sleeping there for a few nights. They sat down and began to talk.

"What's up? Are you okay?"

Vanessa grabbed Kelly and gave her a hug. Kelly began to cry and said, "He is cheating on me. Dan is cheating on me with another woman."

Kim asked, "How do you know he's cheating?"

"I know. I can feel it," said Kelly. "He doesn't come home from work. I found text messages on his phone from her, and he hasn't touched me in a while. He lies and tells me the texts are from his coworkers. He works late into the morning most nights. I don't believe a word that comes out of his lying mouth, and if he's not getting it from me, he's getting it somewhere else."

"Have you caught him with this woman?" asked Kim.

"No, but they're texting back and forth," said Kelly. "I'm thinking about following him to see where he's going."

Vanessa said, "I can't believe he would cheat on you."

Kelly began to cry and became angry and said to Kim, "Where would your cheating man take you? A cheap hotel?"

Kim's mouth dropped open. "Why are you coming at me like that? I'm not the one cheating with your husband. You need to find her and stop coming at me." Kelly and Kim continued going back and forth, yelling at each other.

Vanessa said, "Come on, Kim, it's time to go." She hugged Kelly, and they walked out the door. Vanessa asked Kim if she wanted to come over her house.

Kim said, "Not tonight. I have to meet Mike."

That night, Mike and Kim made passionate love. Kim told him she loved him but couldn't do this anymore and wouldn't take his wife harassing her anymore either. She asked him to leave his wife. Mike got angry. He sat up in the bed and put both of his hands over his head. Then he said he couldn't leave his wife. He got up and put his clothes on, and angrily he said he had to go. Kim lay crying in the bad, feeling foolish for allowing this to continue and go this far and to have stayed in this relationship as long as she had. Mike yelled and said he didn't want to talk about it anymore and walked out, slamming the door behind him. Kim cried even harder.

THE FACE OF BETRAYAL

The next day was the weekend, and Kim hadn't heard from Mike or anyone for that matter. She stayed in bed, crying all day. Meanwhile, Vanessa and Kelly reached out to her to come out with them to get their nails done and a movie. Kim declined saying she didn't feel up to it. The girls decided not to get their nails done and to pick up some food and take it over to Kim's house. They arrived at Kim's house with drinks and food. When they arrived, they found Kim still in bed.

Vanessa said, "Get up. We are having girls' night. Right here, right now."

Kelly went into the kitchen to grab plates and glasses, and she turned on the music. They talked to Kim and began to dish the food and pour the drinks. Kelly made a joke, saying, "I see why you are still lying down. Mike must have blown your back out."

They all looked at each other and began laughing. Kim laughed so hard she began to cry. Vanessa hugged Kim and said, "Sorry about the other day."

Kim said, "Me too."

They sat down and began to eat and talk, and Kim exposed her secret to them, saying she was pregnant by Mike and his wife was harassing her.

"Oh my god," said Vanessa. "This has to stop before someone gets hurt. This is dangerous."

Kelly said, "You have to leave him alone before somebody really gets hurt."

Kim said, "I know, but it's so complicated. I love him, and he is all I know. I put so much time into this relationship. I would leave, but my heart won't let me. I don't know what to do."

"What about the baby?" asked Kelly.

"What did he say?" asked Kelly. "What is he going to do?"

"I don't know, 'cause I haven't told him." Kim turned to Kelly. "What are you going to do about your situation?"

"I don't know," said Kelly, "but I'm not giving up without a fight. He's my best friend and the father of my children, my husband."

Vanessa said, "We may not know what to do, but God does. Let's pray, 'cause I know prayer changes things and people." Each one went into prayer for one another's situation. Later they each returned to their own home.

When Kelly got home, Dan was sitting in the living room in the dark. Kelly walked in and came right to the point. "What is going on, Dan? Are you cheating on me with another woman?"

Dan looked at her and laughed and said, "I'm not cheating on you, you're tripping."

Kelly asked, "Who are you texting at night?"

"It's a coworker," said Dan. "I don't have time for this."

He walked away. Kelly stayed there for a few minutes, thinking to herself, *I don't believe him, not a word that comes out of his lying mouth.* So the next day, Kelly went back to Vanessa and Kim and told them what Dan said. She got so upset, she began to cry. So Kim and Vanessa assured Kelly that whichever way it turned out she'd be all right. Saying the truth would come to the light, and it would reveal itself.

Strange Looks

The next day at work, Vanessa sat in her office, and the boss, Mr. Davis, walked in. He said he would like to talk to her if she had a minute.

"Sure," said Vanessa. "Come in. Have a seat."

Mr. Davis began by saying how pleased he was with Vanessa's work.

"Thank you," said Vanessa, feeling flattered, but there was something about the way he looked at her.

Mr. Davis continued by asking what part of the South she was from.

Vanessa responded, "Surehill."

He went on asking personal questions like, "Are you married?" "Do you have kids?" "Are you dating anyone?"

Vanessa was beginning to feel uncomfortable with his questioning and asked Mr. Davis, "Is there something wrong?"

Mr. Davis responded, "No, everything's fine, real fine." He looked at her as if he could see right through her clothing.

"Is that all, Mr. Davis?" asked Vanessa. I'd really like to get back to work alone.

Mr. Davis smiled and said, "I'll see you later," then winked at her with a strange smile on his face and walked out the door.

Vanessa got up and shut her door behind him. She walked back to her desk, thinking, *What was that all about?* She continued on working. Later that afternoon, she called to check on Kelly. They talked for a while, and she asked Kelly how things were going with Dan.

"Okay, I guess," said Kelly. "But I'm serious about following him to see where he goes."

Vanessa told Kelly, "Those who go looking find things they wish they never found." She asked Kelly, "If you go looking, are you prepared to deal with what you find?"

"I don't know," said Kelly. "But I have to do something. It's driving me crazy not knowing anything."

Vanessa changed the conversation and invited Kelly to have lunch with her and Kim. Kelly declined and said she would catch up with them later. She hung up the phone.

Vanessa grabbed her bags and started down to the cafeteria for lunch. Kim was sitting there on her phone, texting as always. Vanessa ordered her food and sat down at the table.

"Hey, boo!" said Kim, looking up from her phone.

"Hey," said Vanessa.

"What's going on with you today?" said Kim.

"Strange, but Mr. Davis came to my office to talk to me today."

"What happened?" asked Kim.

"I don't know. He wanted to let me know how please he was with my work."

"So?" said Kim.

"And asking me all these personal questions. But it was how he looked at me like, as if he could see through my clothes or something, and that creepy smile he gave me."

Kim started laughing. "You go, girl!" she said jokingly.

Now Mr. Davis wasn't a bad-looking man. He was tall, bright-skinned, built, and a well-dressed man with lovely white teeth. He was not bad on the eyes at all. Kim looked at Vanessa and smiled. Vanessa thought to herself, *Maybe it wasn't anything to worry about.*

Just then, Ruby, an older heavy-set, dark-skinned woman, one of the coworkers, walked over to the table and said, "Hello, ladies!" They said hello. She looked at Vanessa and said, "I see Mr. Davis came to visit your office today," but it was how she said it. "Be careful child!" Then she walked away with a strange look on her face, which made Vanessa feel some kind of way. Chills came over her body. They both looked at each other.

Vanessa said, "Anyway, I talked with Kelly, and she was still talking about following Dan."

Kim looked upward in into the sky and said "Lord!"

At the closing of day, Vanessa looked up from her desk, and standing at the door was Mr. Davis.

"Hope I didn't interrupt you," said Mr. Davis, "but I need to know if you could work overtime tomorrow night. Got a big case I'm working on and could use your help."

Vanessa didn't hesitate; she could use the extra hours. Vanessa said, "No problem."

"Tomorrow then," said Mr. Davis. "Good night."

Vanessa didn't stop by Kelly's house on the way home. She was tired and needed a hot shower and a bed. She would call Kelly before she went to sleep. Vanessa got into the house, taking off her shoes, and headed for the shower. As she got into bed and comfortable, she called Kelly.

"Hey, sweetie. How's it going?"

"It's going so well the kids are in bed, and Dan is downstairs doing paperwork," said Kelly.

"So all's well then?" sad Vanessa.

"As well as is," said Kelly.

Vanessa heard something in Kelly's voice that told her that Kelly had something in her mind that she wasn't ready to share yet. "Are you okay?" said Vanessa.

"I'm okay," said Kelly. Vanessa didn't push but left it alone. Kelly said, "Okay, good night," and hung up.

That night, Kelly lay thinking, *I have two houses to show, and after that, I'll have some time tomorrow to stop by Dan's job and see where it is he is going.*

Kelly was a realtor, so her days were not always full days. She had some time on her hands. After the showing of the houses, she could use to investigate Dan's work habits. Kelly said, "I'll find out what Dan is up to." She turned off the lights and went to sleep. Dan was downstairs on the phone, talking to someone telling them he would meet them for lunch tomorrow. He hung up the phone, made himself a drink, and sat on the couch in a daze. He had no idea that Kelly heard his conversation. Once he was finished his drink, he went to bed.

PRAYING IN THE MIST OF CHAOS

Kim took the day off and did not talk to anyone today. She was lying in her bed all day, crying and trying to figure out what to do about Mike and the child she was carrying. She hadn't talk to Mike in a few days now. She thought to herself what it would be like for her and Mike to be together and raise a family.

The next day, Vanessa showed up to work, feeling really good. She was not sure why, but it felt good. She and Kim met in the hallway. Kim said, "Hey, how's it going?"

Vanessa said, "I don't know, you tell me! Is everything okay?"

Kim noticed Roberta, one of the coworkers, was staring in her mouth, being nosy. She said, "I can't stand people looking in my mouth. We'll talk at lunch." She rolled her eyes at Roberta and walked away. Vanessa looked around, and sure enough, Roberta was all in the business.

Now the word has been out that Roberta had a fling with the boss, Mr. Davis, but Vanessa could care less because she wasn't there for the gossip. She walked into her office and started to work on the files on her desk.

By midday, Kim got a visit from Mike's wife, and the drama took place. Hands were thrown, and threats were made. Nikki, Mike's wife, told Kim to stay away from her husband or she would be sorry she ever met him. Rumor was going around that Nikki wasn't playing with a full deck and she was crazy and even crazier when it came to Mike. Now Nikki has caused the uproar in the office. Security had to be called and Nikki put out and told if she came back into that building, she would be arrested.

Cops arrived, and Kim had to go downtown to file complaint and put a restraining order on Nikki. Kim was frantically yelling at Mike to pick up the phone. She was yelling into the phone machine, telling what is happening, cursing and crying and going crazy. Things calmed down. Vanessa and Kelly told Kim to stay away from Mike before somebody really gets hurt badly. Kim finally got it and stopped calling and seeing Mike, putting a restraint on both Nikki and Mike.

THE RUBBER MEETS THE ROAD

Kim told Vanessa and Kelly she hadn't seen or heard from Mike, and Nikki didn't believe her and still was harassing her.

Vanessa was returning to her office when she noticed a tall dark-skinned woman coming out of Mr. Davis's office. By the way he kissed her, she realized it was his wife, Shirley. Vanessa went into her office and began doing some paperwork, then she heard a knock on the door. She looked up to see Mr. Davis standing in the doorway. He asked her if she was done with the work they had to do tonight.

"Yes, I'm finishing up the paperwork now."

Mr. Davis said okay and smiled and winked at her and walked away. As he walked away, she remembered she didn't let Kim know she wouldn't need the ride tonight. She would be working late, so she texted Kim and Kim sent her back a smiley face and said "Be careful." That seemed to bother Vanessa.

Why does everyone keep saying be careful? Careful for what? Vanessa thought. Vanessa looked up from her desk. She felt someone staring at her. It was Roberta sitting at her desk, looking at Vanessa like she had something to say. Vanessa looked back at her like "What?" Roberta turned away. At the end of the day, everyone was going home for the night. Vanessa was worried about Kim and what had taken place earlier with Nikki, but she prayed God's protection over Kim and continued to work. Now she felt someone standing in the doorway.

"You frighten me. I didn't hear you coming toward me," said Vanessa. It was Mr. Davis.

He smiled and said, "But you can feel me coming in you," with a creepy laugh in a wink.

"Excuse me?" said Vanessa. She heard what he said, but she wanted him to repeat it. But she knew she heard him correctly. He continued.

"Just coming to check in on you," said Mr. Davis. He came in closer behind her chair. Vanessa felt strange with him creeping over her, then she felt his breath on her neck.

She thought, *I know he didn't just smell my hair*. Vanessa stood up and turned around and asked, "Is there something I can do for you, Mr. Davis? If not, I rather work alone."

He put his hands up and surrender Mode and said good night and then walked out. She sat down and thought to herself, *He tried it*. She continued to finish up at work at the close of the night Mr. Davis walked by on his way home. Vanessa packed her things and went home. Vanessa couldn't sleep that night. Every time she closed her eyes, she would envision a group of women who seemed to be broken and in pain and in tears. She didn't understand why God kept showing her this. She saw Kim, Kelly, Roberta, and other women she did not know. She got up made a pot of tea, hoping it would soothe her to sleep, and it sure did. She had a peaceful sleep that night.

BETRAYAL

Kelly, feeling lost and betrayed, decided she was going to follow Dan and see what he had been up to. That morning, Kelly kissed Dan goodbye as he headed out to work. Kelly dropped the kids off to school. She drove thinking to herself. Vanessa's voice in her head asked if she would be prepared for what she might find. Despite whether she was ready or not, she decided to follow Dan around, watching and waiting his every move. Around lunchtime Dan got into his car and headed to a restaurant. There he entered and got a table in the booth. A few seconds later, a beautiful woman walked in and joined him in the booth. As she walked up, Dan stood up and embraced and kissed her. They sat down and began to talk.

On seeing this, Kelly began to cry, and she became very angry. She wanted to get out and rip off their faces off, but a little voice inside of her told her to keep her peace, and she did. She pulled out and spent off returning home. Once home, she found herself in fetal position, crying even harder, wondering how her husband could do this to her. Then the phone rang. It was Kim.

"Are you okay?" asked Kim. Kelly just cried into the phone. "I'll be right there," said Kim. She hung up the phone and called Vanessa. "It's Kelly. Something's wrong with Kelly." Vanessa hung up and ran to Mr. Davis's office. She expressed she had an emergency and had to go home. Mr. Davis okayed it, and Vanessa headed over to Kelly's house. As Vanessa ran Kim followed behind her as they headed to the door to ring the bell. Kelly didn't respond. They walked in to find Kelly in fetal position on the floor, crying. Seeing Kelly hurt like this made them angry. Kelly was yelling about killing Dan and the woman he was with. Listening to how deeply she hurt inside, they all ended up hugging up crying on the floor.

While in this position, Vanessa realized that was what she saw in the vision that night, but she still didn't understand the meaning. Pulling themselves together, they realized they all needed to cry that thing out. And now the question was "What would they do now?" They discussed the next steps of action to be taken. Vanessa began to pray about each and every situation one by one. She prayed to God for peace of heart and mind for all and for God to reveal his will and the power to carry it out. Vanessa looked at each of them and said, "Now we wait and trust God to do what only God could do."

That night, they had a sleepover, kids and all, at Vanessa's house. They watched movies and enjoyed each other's company.

When Kelly didn't return home, Dan called Kelly's phone several times only to get no response. Dan became worried with fear all thoughts of Kelly and the kids flood his brain as he began knocking on Vanessa's door. Finally, Vanessa said, "Dan, I'm going to ask you to step away from my door and go home before I have to call the cops and tell them you're harassing us. I'm sure if you give Kelly some time, she'll call you."

Dan hesitantly walked away and headed back home. Once in the house, he decided to have a drink and noticed a letter from Kelly telling him she followed him and knew what he did. Now Dan was frantically bugging out. Now he needed to talk to Kelly to explain, but she wouldn't talk to him. Dan was frantic thinking Kelly knew everything. He called his friend Lamar to tell him all that had happened. Lamar told Dan to calm down because everything would be all right. And if all came down to it, they would both tell their wives together. Then Lamar told Dan to meet him at their spot and hung up. Dan decided to have another drink and headed to meet Lamar, but Dan had an accident on the way to meet Lamar. Dan ended up in the hospital in a bad condition, not able to move or talk. The hospital called Kelly to inform her that her husband had been in a car accident. Kelly, in shock, now needed to get to the hospital. Vanessa went with her. They arrived, and the nurse took Kelly to her husband's room. Kelly was still angry with Dan, but when she saw him in this condition, she had compassion on him. Meanwhile, Lamar found out about Dan's accident while watching the news. He felt the need to be there for Dan.

UNVEILING SECRETS

But what Lamar didn't know was that his wife, Roberta, had been following him and was outside watching and waiting his next move. Lamar knew he shouldn't go to the hospital but ended up going anyway. He jumped in the car and pulled out, headed toward the hospital, not realizing his wife was right behind him. He showed up just as Kelly stepped out of the room for a minute.

Lamar entered Dan's room. When he saw Dan's condition, he cried out, expressing his love for Dan. Dan, not being able to move or speak, had tears in his eyes and just looked at Lamar with this crazy look. Lamar continued talking about their affair, expressing his love for Dan. Unknowingly, Kelly was standing in the door, listening in awe, and Lamar's wife was standing right next to her. Roberta and Kelly, both with tears in their eyes, were in disbelief. Vanessa was wondering if she was mistaken when she thought she saw Roberta enter the hospital. She walked to the back to see if she could find her. The nurse walked in the room and said to Kelly, "I have your husband's blood work back." The nurse asked Dan, "Are you aware you are positive for HIV?" Kelly screamed so loud Vanessa heard it and came running. Kelly was gone with it. She was out of it. As Vanessa ran up just in time to catch Kelly, she lost her footing, fainting into Vanessa's arms. Roberta stood there in shock and tears running down her face. As Lamar lay crying on Dan's chest, the nurse became aware of what was going on. She said, "You all need to be tested." Vanessa, now holding Kelly, reached out to Roberta and held her, and they cried.

CONFUSION

That night, there was nothing but confusion in the air. Kelly took some time off work and stayed home, trying to figure things out. While Kelly was sitting on the couch, the doorbell rang. She opened the door to find the woman she had seen with Dan at the restaurant.

What the hell is she doing here? Kelly thought herself. She opened the door with a confused look on her face. "Can I help you?" said Kelly.

The woman said, "My name is Rita, attorney. Your husband hired me. Can I come in and talk to you?"

"Come in," said Kelly. They sat down. Kelly said, "I saw you with my husband at the restaurant. I'm confused why you're here."

Rita said, "Yes, he asked me to meet him to go over some divorce papers."

Kelly became angry. "Divorce papers, really?"

"Yes, I have the papers with me." She handed Kelly the divorce papers and said, "I must be leaving now." Kelly walked her out and closed the door behind her.

Kelly thought to herself, *This Negro has lost his mind.* She made a drink and started to put things together. The phone rang. It was Roberta wanting to meet with Kelly and talk. They decided to schedule a meet date for next week. That night, Kim and Vanessa came over, and they had discussion about everything that had been happening. Kim informed them that she would be keeping the baby. Despite Nikki's harassment there was an upside to things Kim decided to keep her baby and was even started to show. They were all happy with her decision and supported her all the way. Kim had accepted that she would have this baby with or without Mike's help. Kim glowed as she spoke about her morning sickness and her eating habits. The girls were pleased that Kim decided to keep the baby, and they couldn't wait for the baby's arrival. Vanessa's phone rang. That was Mr. Davis asking if Vanessa could do some overtime to finish up the case. Vanessa didn't mind. She said yes. She needed extra money. Mr. Davis said, "Great," and hung up.

Kelly began to cry and said she didn't know why she didn't pay attention to all the signs that was given her. "And there were many signs," said Kelly.

Vanessa responded to Kelly, "Perhaps you didn't want to see the signs. He was your husband."

"But he betrayed me," said Kelly.

Vanessa asked, "What will happen when he's released from the hospital?"

Kelly said, "He wants a divorce. He shall have it," asked Kim, "and I don't care what happens to him. I said I'm packing his things and I don't care where we take them."

"What about the kids? Have you talked to them yet?" Vanessa asked.

"Talk to them yet?" asked Vanessa.

"Not yet," said Kelly, "but God will make a way, and we'll get through this. The kids knew about Dan's accident, but that is all they know for now."

Vanessa asked Kim, "What about Mike? Have you seen or heard from him?"

"No, I haven't, but I did hear he found another chick, and I say God bless them."

Kelly said, "I talked with Roberta, and she wants to get together to talk."

The girls said, "That's great."

NEW ASSIGNMENT

Well, at work, Vanessa was sitting at her desk, and she felt a presence in the room. She looked up to find Shirley standing in the doorway. She said, "We haven't met. I'm Mrs. Davis." Vanessa stood up and extended her hand out to greet Mrs. Davis. She looked down at Vanessa's hand and looked back up at her with such a nasty look on her face and said, "You are not as pretty as Mr. Davis thinks you are." Then she walked away, leaving Vanessa just standing there with her mouth open, standing in the doorway, thinking, *What was that about?*

Vanessa sat back down at her desk and began to work. Later that afternoon, Mr. Davis asked Vanessa to come to his office. When she arrived, there stood Mr. Davis and another gentleman she hadn't met. He was a very good-looking man, brown skin, strong build, hazel eyes, and a lovely bright smile. Mr. Davis said, "This is Carl. He's a nice guy. You will be working with him starting next week on a new case. Now this job will require some late night as well, if you are interested."

Vanessa said, "Sure, that sounds great."

"Okay then," said Mr. Davis, "finish up what you're working on, and you'll start your new case next week. Good day."

Vanessa walked out. When she reached her office, she sat down at her desk. She thought about how nice-looking Carl was, what it would be like to work with him. Vanessa picked up the phone to call Kelly, who had been at the hospital all day with Dan. When the phone rang, Kelly had just entered the laundry room.

"Hey," Kelly said. "Vanessa, what's up with you? Have you talked to Kim?"

37

"No, but I'm supposed to meet her for lunch. Hey, Mr. Davis just gave me a new assignment," said Vanessa. "I start next week."

"Great," said Kelly. "Congratulations."

"Thanks," said Vanessa. "I'll talk to you later." They hung up.

STRANGE VIBES

Vanessa started to tidy up her desk before lunch. As she walked down the hall toward the cafeteria, she saw Roberta wearing dark shades, looking strange. When Vanessa looked in Roberta's direction, she put her head down. Vanessa continued to walk past her toward the cafeteria. As she entered, she saw Kim sitting at the table, eating. She got her lunch and walked to the table and sat down. She noticed her coworkers Trina and Jenny; they seemed upset.

Vanessa asked Kim, "What's with them?"

Kim said, "Who? Mr. Davis's girls?"

Vanessa said, "What? What does that mean?"

Vanessa just looked away and said, "Ask him. So how are you doing, belly?" They both laughed, and Kim responded by telling Vanessa that her feet were swollen and she felt like she was carrying a thousand pounds.

"This baby got me going. What about you? How is it going?" asked Kim.

"Well, Mr. Davis has given me a new assignment for next week with this guy name Carl."

"Wow, you're going to be working with Carl?" asked Kim. "Wow, that's the stuff," said Kim. "He's the head honcho."

"What does that mean?" asked Vanessa.

"He's the man, and that's all you need to know! He is fine as hell and single. He's a nice-looking man who all the women's staff been trying to get with him," said Kim. "And nothing until now!" They laughed.

"Okay then! By the way, I saw Roberta on the way down here, and she was wearing some shades."

"That asshole has put his hands on her again," said Kim.

"Again?" asked Vanessa.

"Yes, he beats on her every chance he gets."

"That is so sad," said Vanessa.

Kim changed the subject. "How is Kelly?"

"She has been at the hospital all day with Dan. She's home now, packing his things and cleaning. Dan seems to be doing okay. He's doing therapy now."

Kim said, "I still can't believe he cheated on her, with a man at that."

Vanessa said, "You can't help who you love."

"Amen," said Kim. "When do they get their test back?" asked Kim.

"Sometime next week."

"I'm praying for them," said Kim.

"Me too," said Vanessa.

Kim asked, "When are we meeting with Roberta?"

"Next week," responded Vanessa. "At Kelly's house after work. Okay, I'm going back to work."

"See you later," said Kim. Vanessa didn't see Kim anymore that day. She would be working late, finishing up the work with Mr. Davis.

Kim had taken the day off and hadn't talked to anyone all day. Feeling kind of tired, she stayed in the bed. She only left her bedroom to eat. She got up and went into the kitchen to make some tea, hoping it would help her to sleep, and sure enough, the tea makes her sleepy. As she slept, she dreamed the same dream she had been having for the last few nights. The woman in the dream wore dark clothing and head covering, and all Kim could see was her eyes.

Kim heard a sound downstairs, but she wasn't sure if it was a part of the dream. As she slowly opened her eyes and listened, she realized it wasn't a part of the dream. She headed downstairs staring out at her. It was dark, and the light switch was at the end of the stairs, so she grabbed the flashlight. She headed downstairs. As she reached the bottom step, she was hit on the head and knocked out. When she awoke, she had no idea how long she had been out, but she woke up to a woman dressed in dark clothing and piercing eyes.

Kim began to struggle to get up but Nikki pushed her back down. Kim pleaded with Nikki but she ignored her. Kim crawled down the hallway towards the kitchen near the downstairs bathroom. Kim was bleeding but didn't know where it all was coming from. She crawled to the bathroom and locked herself in. She was stabbed and cut everywhere. Seeing all the blood made her feel faint. She could hear Nikki barely yelling and banging on the door, stabbing at the door. She was throwing and breaking things in the house.

Nikki was yelling that she was going to kill Kim and her baby, and Kim passed out. She first heard glass breaking and things going around, then it went black. She passed out. The phone was ringing. It just continued to ring and ring and ring. It was Kelly trying to contact Kim, but the phone just rang. After no response, Kelly called Vanessa. Vanessa told Kelly about an incident with Mr. Davis. Kelly was angry, then asked if she had spoken with Kim. Kelly explained she called Kim and got no answer. The following day, they were to meet up with Roberta at Kelly's house.

GOD STEPS IN

That morning, Vanessa reported to work, hoping not to run into Mr. Davis. As she walked toward her office, she noticed Mr. Davis's office door was closed. Vanessa walked into her office and shut the door behind her. As she sat at her desk, flashbacks of the incident with Mrs. Davis flooded her mind. To get things off her mind, she picked up the phone to call Kim, but no answer. So she continued making other calls and doing paperwork.

As the day went on, she realized she still hadn't heard anything from Mr. Davis someone knocked on the door. It was Carl. He said, "Just checking in on you, making sure you are okay." Then he said, "Mr. Davis is in a meeting with the board and wouldn't be back in today."

Vanessa thought to herself, no wonder she hadn't seen him. It was lunchtime now, and she realized she heard from Kim either. She packed up her things and headed down toward the cafeteria, thinking she would see Kim there as always, but when she arrived and didn't see Kim, she became worried. She also asked Raberta if she seen Kim today.

"Roberta," she responded. "She didn't come in today."

Vanessa called Kim again. No answer. She called Kelly and said, "Kim is still not answering, and she's not at work." Kelly said she would go over and check on Kim. Vanessa said, "Okay, call me back."

When Kelly arrived at Kim's house, she noticed Kim's car was there. She walked up to the door and rang the bell. She began to knock and bang on the door, yelling Kim's name then she walked around toward the windows, but she couldn't see anything. The curtains were pulled close. She tried calling again. No response. She returned the call to Vanessa and explained that Kim's car was parked at the house but she was getting no response from Kim.

Vanessa said she would call the police and meet Kelly there. Vanessa went to Mr. Davis's office and knocked on the door to let Carl know she had to leave because she had an emergency. Carl gave Vanessa the okay to leave. Vanessa got a ride with Roberta, heading to Kim's house.

As Vanessa and Roberta arrived at Kim's house, they saw Kelly pacing back and forth at Kim's door. They rushed to Kelly. As they came together, the police arrived, and they explained to the police that they were worried about their friend. She didn't report to work, and they had been calling her and getting no response. They showed them that her car was still parked. The police now had to break the door down. As they entered the house, they found it in disarray—furniture thrown around, broken glass everywhere. Then they found blood by the stairs.

Kelly ran upstairs, yelling Kim's name. Vanessa moved about the house downstairs, calling out for Kim. Vanessa realized the bathroom door was locked and called out for help. Everyone ran to where Vanessa was. The cops found blood on the bathroom door and asked Kelly and Vanessa to back up from the door and enter the other room. While they were entering the other room, the cops broke the bathroom door down, finding Kim barely breathing on the floor in a puddle of blood.

The ladies become very frantic, screaming and crying, trying to get to Kim, wanting badly to know if she was alive, but the cops would tell them nothing. The cops called in for emergency responders and could barely hear from all the screaming the ladies were doing. Roberta asked if Kim was alive but got no response from the cops. Kelly's mind kept going back to all the blood Kim was lying in. The emergency responders finally got Kim to the hospital.

Vanessa, Kelly, and Roberta were waiting in the ER to get word on Kim's condition. While waiting at the hospital with everyone crying, Vanessa said, "The best thing we can do for Kim is pray to the Father God that he will bring Kim through this."

Vanessa, Kelly, and Roberta grabbed hands and began to pray over the doctor's hands, over Kim, and her baby's life. Finally, a doctor came out and said, "Kim came out of surgery, but she is not out of the woods yet. We must wait and see how she is when she awakens."

Kelly asked about the baby. He said, "It appears the baby's fine." Vanessa asked if they could see Kim. The doctor said, "Yes, but not tonight. Maybe tomorrow when she's feeling up to it." Then he said, "You ladies should go home and get some rest."

Relieved, they hugged each other and thanked God for all that he had done. They began to walk out of the hospital. As they got to their cars, they departed and went their own ways home. When Kelly got home, she realized she had messages on her phone. One of them was from Dan's doctor, reporting Dan's improvements. She said he would be released in a few days and that she would talk further with Kelly about the blood test when she came in to see Dan. This message made Kelly feel uneasy. Dealing with Dan and getting the results from the HIV test were very unsettling.

The bell rang. It was Kelly's mom dropping the kids off. She opened the door; the kids ran in and gave her kisses and hugs and ran directly to their rooms. Kelly had it in her mind that she would tell the kids about her and their dad getting divorced tonight. Her mom walked in and asked how Kim was doing.

"We don't know anything yet, Mom," said Kelly, waving her mom in to have a seat while Kelly went into the kitchen to make them drinks. Kelly handed her mom a drink and sat down.

Her mom looked at Kelly and said, "How are you doing?"

Kelly said, "I'm going crazy, Mom, with all this."

Her mom asked Kelly, "Did you tell the kids yet?"

"I don't feel like I can tell them tonight, Mom."

Her mom said, "When you're ready, I'll be there for support."

Kelly said, "Thanks, Mom."

"I pray for Kim and her baby that they'll be all right." Her mom got up and walked toward the door and said, "Kelly, if you need me, I'm a phone call away." They hugged and kissed, and her mom left. Kelly finished her drink and went to her bedroom.

Roberta walked into her house and found Lamar in the dining room, having a drink. It seemed he had more than one drink. He looked up at her, and neither of them said a word to the other. Roberta went to the bathroom, sat on her bed, and prayed, "God, give me the strength to do what needs to be done."

Lamar and Roberta also had to see the doctor for their results as well, both feeling some kind of way about what they might or might not learn tomorrow. Roberta decided she would take a shower and go to bed, but before she did, she went to check on her children. She went to each of their rooms, giving each a kiss goodnight.

The next day, Roberta and Lamar headed to the doctor for their results. The doctor talked to them together. She told Lamar that he was positive for HIV and gave him a prescription for medication. Then she told Roberta she was negative for HIV but positive for pregnancy. By the looks of things, maybe five or almost six months. At the sound of this news, Roberta's and Lamar's mouths dropped open. Roberta thought to herself, *I just thought I was getting fat.* The doctor gave her a prescription for vitamins in the name of a doctor for prenatal care. They both walked out of the office, puzzled, and went their own ways.

Roberta began to reminisce, thinking to herself the timelines up from the time that Mr. Davis raped her. She said to herself, *Mr. Davis is my baby daddy?* She felt sick. She thought about all the sickness and the throwing up she had done, and thought she caught a bug or something. As she walked down the hall, Roberta ran into Kelly on her way to check on Kim, Kelly was already there to see Dan. Kelly arrived to see Dan. The doctor came in the room and said, "I would like to see you both in my office."

She said, "I have your results back. Dan is doing very well with therapy. Unfortunately, there are still some limits in walking, so he'll be using a cane. Also, he needs to continue therapy, but he will be able to go home in a few days. Unfortunately, his results showed he was positive for HIV." She said she would start him on medication. "Dan showed no emotion he just sat in silence." She said, "Kelly your results show you are negative for HIV but positive for type 2 diabetes, and as such, you will have to take insolent daily."

The doctor gave Kelly a pamphlet on diabetes and also gave her a prescription for insulin and a doctor that specialized in diabetic patients. She gave Dan the number for a HIV doctor. She said, "I suggest that you and your family get some counseling." She gave Kelly a number for family counseling and said good luck with everything.

Dan was taken back to his room, and Kelly walked back down the hall to see Kim. As she walked into Kim's room, they all greeted each other. Kelly asked Kim how she was feeling. Kim responded, "I'm all right now." Then the questions came from everywhere.

"How is the baby?" asked Vanessa.

"It's a girl, and we're both fine. She should be arriving any day now," said Kim. "The doctors will be doing a C-section due to the incident, and I have to have surgery."

Roberta asked, "What happened?"

Kim explained that Nikki must have gotten a hold of Mike's keys him, and she never changed the locks. "Nikki's still thinking that I am messing with Mike, but I haven't seen Mike. She came into my house while I was sleeping. I heard something downstairs. I went to check it out she hit me over the head and knocked me out, and all I know she was stabbing me with a knife." Kim began to show them where Nikki stabbed her and all her bruises. One particular area was where Nikki hit a nerve in her legs, and if they would not do surgery, Kim would never walk again.

"Everyone was happy Kim and the baby were alright, and Kelly's test came back negative. And also, they were shocked about Roberta's baby. But glad about her decision to devoice Lamar. The ladies trusted in God that all would be well. Then the nurse came and said visitors must leave. Kim needed her rest. They left Kim to get rest.

BONDING IN PAIN

Later that evening, the women went over to Vanessa's house. Roberta and Kelly arrived at the same time. Vanessa made them a drink. Kelly sat down and began to talk about what had taken place in the last few days. They were all pleased that Kim's baby was all right but worried about the surgery and C-section Kim would have to undergo. As they continued to talk, the doorbell rang. It was Trina and Jenny. They were concerned hearing what happened to Kim. They had gone to see her at the hospital. They returned to Vanessa's house. Vanessa told them to come in and have a seat while she made them drinks.

The conversations continued. Trina was very irritated about what happened to Kim and said, "I knew it had to be that crazy-ass Nikki who did that to Kim, and I told the officers that she had threatened Kim."

Jenny said, "Yeah, they finally picked her up and took her ass to jail. They charged her with attempted murder, and all this over dumbass Mike."

Trina asked, "Did you hear what happened to Mr. Davis? The board has fired him, and now he's under investigation for harassment and three counts of rape." Trina said, "He raped me last year." In shock, all the ladies' mouths dropped wide open. "He threatened me to keep my mouth shut if I wanted to keep my job, and he said no one would believe me anyway." She began to cry.

Roberta hugged Trina and said, "Yeah, he raped me."

Then Jenny said, "He raped me, too, and told me if I tell anyone, he would tell them that I came on to him, and I would lose my job." She also began cry.

Kelly gave her a hug, then Roberta said, "He raped me, too, and I'm just finding out that I'm pregnant. He's the daddy." The shock in the room.

Vanessa went to Trina and said, "I'm sorry I yelled at you the other night. I didn't realize that you were trying to warn me about Mr. Davis. He tried to rape me that night, but thank God for Carl being in the building. He rescued me from him." She told the ladies everything that happened that night. She said, "He must be stopped, and each of us has been raped in one way or another. Being women, we need to stick together 'cause we don't know how many other women are out there that he's done this to. The board has investigated Mr. Davis. He's unaware of this, and they will want to speak to each of us about this. I would hope you would all come forward." The women agreed. They were about to form a sisterhood, and they would call themselves Women of Encouragement.

Roberta discussed her marriage to Lamar. She began by saying he was her first and only partner—except for the rape of course. They had been together since high school, and he was her best friend and the father of her two children. As she continued to talk, her story sounded so much like Kelly's story. She spoke of how it all began and when it all went wrong. She didn't know what to think now. She was feeling so confused and stupid, thinking of all the signs that were there, and she ignored them. Now she wished that Lamar was cheating with a woman. Kelly also wished Dan had been with a woman and not a man. Kelly said she was glad she found out now, because she was going crazy not knowing anything. She only wished she knew earlier. Kelly said that she and her kids would get counseling and move on, and she packed Dan's things and had found him an apartment that he would move into when he was released from the hospital.

Kelly told Roberta that she had a good divorce lawyer and handed her a card with the name and number. "Give her a call," said Kelly. "Her name is Rita, and she will take care of you."

Roberta said, "Lamar packed his things and moved out already. He texted me and said he was going to a hotel. Thank God."

The women decided to meet up again next week, same time and place. A woman would also be there next week to talk to them about the rape case. It was good now that Nikki and Mr. Davis were behind bars. The women closed the meeting in prayer. Vanessa began by praying for Kim and the baby, and each one prayed for the others' situations. After the prayer, all felt better knowing they weren't alone anymore now they had each other and would be strengthened and lifted up in prayer and in life. God had begun a bond with these women, and it was not going to be easily broken. These women had been bent but not broken, and with each other's help, they would stand together for the journey ahead with God leading them all the way.

VISION

Later that night, Vanessa realized what took place with the women was what God had been showing her in the vision, and it was manifesting right before her eyes. She felt good in spirit and continued to thank God for such a blessing. She could hear God's voice saying these words, "Women of Encouragement," and she could envision her mom's face for the first time since she had passed away, just smiling at her with a pleased look on her face. She was saying, "Women of Encouragement, that's who you are. It's your purpose to encourage women through God's leading."

LETTING GOD LEAD

Kelly said, "This calls for a celebration. Why don't we get together later tonight?"

All agreed. Kelly walked further down the hall toward Dan's room, where he was waiting to be released from doctor's care.

Kelly asked, "Are you ready to leave?"

Dan was dressed and sitting by the window, and. Dan said, "Yes, get me out of here!" The nurse handed Kelly the discharge papers and prescription and his appointment for therapy, and Kelly wheeled Dan down the hall in a wheelchair. As she got him in the car heading to his new apartment she rented for him, Kelly said they must stop by the house to pick up Dan's things. When they arrived at the house, the children were waiting outside with a few of his things. They loaded the car, and they drove to the apartment, which was not that far from the house but far enough, Kelly thought to herself.

Back at the house, the kids helped Dan out of the car and into the house while Kelly stayed in the car and prayed, "Father, help me to restrain my feeling and to do what is right now as his wife. Give me strength, Lord, to do this as your child. I ask in Jesus's name. Amen!"

Kelly would help Dan out until he got better and was back on his feet. She was angry and had to pray daily to do these things without letting her anger get in the way. The best way she knew how was to say nothing and do what needed to be done and move on. With God's help, she would do this if it was the last thing she did for him. The kids came back to the car to get Dan's bags. Kelly got out and took the bags of food out of the truck. The kids asked if she was all right.

"Yes, I'm good," said Kelly. They walked in the house, and Kelly went into the kitchen and put the food away. She began to prepare dinner, giving Dan time to talk with the kids. She didn't say a word until dinner was ready. They all sat down and prayed over the food. After dinner, Dan finally got a chance to talk to Kelly. Dan apologized to her, telling her everything. He told her when he met Lamar and that when they found out they were positive he and Lamar had gone to be tested a long while ago. When he stopped making love to her, he wanted to tell her, but he didn't know how. It just became so much easier to continue to let her think he was cheating with another woman and why he continued the lie. He never wanted to hurt her and the kids. It was the last thing he ever wanted to do. He figured that divorce would be better for all of them. Dan was glad that she wasn't HIV positive, that he couldn't live with his self if she was. He was sorry he put her through all this and understood if she never forgave him.

Kelly was angry and felt even more betray because he knew all this time and kept her in the dark. She explained he never gave a fuck about her. If he did, he would have told her and given her the opportunity to have a choice. She told Dan she would only do what the Lord laid on her heart to do. She was to help him out until he was better, she said; but after this, she didn't want anything else to do with him!

Kelly would allow Dan to see the kids, but it was over for them. Dan apologized again and said he wouldn't fight for anything in the divorce settlement, that she deserved it all for what he put her through. Kelly called out to the kids, "We are leaving," and walked out the door.

LET GO AND LET GOD

Roberta walked into the lawyer's office. They sat down and began the paperwork. She was very tired, not getting much sleep lately, knowing she would be giving birth soon to her rapist's baby. To Roberta, this all felt like a dream that she couldn't wake up from. On the other hand, her children were happy they would be having another brother or sister. They didn't understanding the circumstances; this baby was a result of the man who hurt their mommy. When Roberta got home, she decided to call and check on Kim, but Kim was still in surgery, so she decided to take a nap.

Being on leave now didn't leave her much to do. And her doctor's appointment wasn't until later that afternoon. The kids were in school. She had the house to herself. She lay down, and before she knew it, she was asleep. Roberta had a dream about a beautiful baby girl who looked so much like Lily, her daughter. She continued to dream of a new home. It was when the dream turned and Mr. Davis's face appeared in the dream. He was saying something, but Roberta couldn't make out what he was saying. She woke up sweating, frightened out of her mind. She didn't know how long she had been sleeping, but it was now time for her doctor's appointment. There wasn't a reason to rush back home because her mom would be picking the kids up from school. She drove down to the doctor's office for her first baby exam. After the examination, Roberta and the doctor sat down.

"You are carrying a healthy baby girl," said the doctor. Roberta was pleased it was a girl. Soon her smile turned into a frown when she thought about Shirley, Mr. Davis's wife, and how Shirley had no idea that she was carrying Mr. Davis's baby, not even that Mr. Davis had raped her.

53

Roberta thought to herself, *How do you tell another woman that her husband raped you and you're carrying his baby?* Roberta had a secret she wanted to tell but didn't know how to tell it, but she felt it was only right that Shirley knew what her husband had done.

MIXED EMOTION

Vanessa and Carl were at the office, working on their new assignment. Vanessa stared at Carl and realized she enjoyed Carl's company, working, talking, laughing. She really enjoyed working with him. She was even spending a lot of time outside of work with Carl. They had even spent late evenings together, and Vanessa was feeling attracted to him. She was beginning to feel the attraction between them and wondered what it would be like if it was more than just business.

Sitting at the desk, the phone rang. It was the hospital nurse informing her that Kim's surgery was successful and that she would be moved to a recovery room and able to have visitors tonight. Vanessa thanked God and thanked the nurse for calling her. She hung up. She looked up to heaven and said, "Thank you, Father." Just then, she was picking up the phone to call Kelly to give her the good news. There was a knock on the door. It was Carl.

He stuck his head in and said, "Can you meet me in my office in an hour?"

"Sure," said Vanessa.

Carl closed the door and walked away. Vanessa sat there for a minute and remembered she had to call Kelly and tell her the news about Kim. She called Kelly, and Kelly was glad to hear the news about Kim. Vanessa and Kelly decided to meet up at the hospital after work. Vanessa continued to work, and in an hour, she reported to Carl's office.

Carl started out asking how Kim was doing and congratulate them on the baby. He said, "I called you in here to discuss the changes going on in this office. Mr. Davis will not be returning with us. The board has asked me to step up to his position, so I will now be president. I will need a vice president, and the board and I would like you to consider this position. Now if you do decide to take it, it will require some training and late nights, and you will also need to find someone to fill your position."

Vanessa's mouth dropped wide open. She couldn't find the words to say. As she did, the phone rang. "Can I get back to you?" said Vanessa.

"Yes, please," said Carl. Carl picked up the receiver. "Hello," said Carl. The person on the other end began to speak, and as Vanessa looked at Carl, his mouth dropped open. He said, "Thank you," and hung up with a puzzled look on his face.

Vanessa asked, "What's the matter?"

"I was just told during the investigation on Nikki that she also killed Mike's first wife and they just found Nikki hanging in her cell. She is dead! I guess all the pressure got to her, and she decided to end it all."

Vanessa sat back with her hands over her mouth, and a tear roll down her face. Vanessa prayed within her heart for Nikki's family and thanked God he spared Kim's life. "Can I call you later?" Carl waved his hand yes, and Vanessa went back to her desk and just set there in silence. The phone rang. It was Roberta.

"Hey, V," said Roberta.

Vanessa said, "What's up, Berta?"

"Girl, my mind is working overtime," said Roberta. "I went to see the divorce lawyer today, and we took care of the paperwork. I also went to the doctor. It's a girl! I'm happy. But I'm having mixed feelings about the circumstances. The child, I'm having my rapist's baby! And all I can think about is his wife, Shirley. She's in the dark, V, and she needs to know what her husband has done. I feel she deserve to know what she's dealing with. Should I tell her, V? If you feel you are in the right head space and can handle the emotional load, then by all means tell her, but you must be prepared for the outcome. Will you come with me?"

"Sure, I'll come with you for support."

"Thank you."

"You're welcome. Anytime. We will talk later."

Vanessa had something she wanted to share with Kim about Nikki, but knowing all the women would be coming to the hospital, she decided to wait until they were all together. She knew Kim would need the emotional support upon hearing this news. There was another knock on the door. It was Carl again letting her know he would also be at the hospital when Kim got this news.

"I know you will all be there in support of Kim, and she could use all our support."

"Of course," said Vanessa. "Thank you. We will see you there."

Carl closed the door and walked away, thinking to himself, *Damn, she is beautiful.*

He smiled and shook his head. That evening at the hospital, they talked to Kim about Nikki. They were also told about Mr. Davis trial, and they would all have to testify. Kim sat there in a puddle of tears, having mixed emotions. The women hugged and consoled her. Then Carl walked over to Kim and gave her a hug and looked around the room. Everyone in the room was in tears. Carl walked out also in tears. The doctor walked in with good news. Kim's surgery went well, and she could go home in a few days with her baby. They were all pleased at this news. They discussed Roberta's decision to tell Shirley about the rape and baby. Kim just sat there, not saying anything, with total confusion on her face. They all agreed Kim should get some rest. They kissed her goodbye.

When Kelly arrived home, she had received a message from the lawyer stating her divorce was final. Also, she had a call from her son's school, asking her to come pick him up. There had been an incident with him and another child. He also hit the principal and was being suspended from school.

Kelly thought to herself, *One step forward, one step back.* She got back into her the car, heading to the school to pick up James. When she walked into the principal's office, she heard loud yelling and cursing and saw tears running down James's face. James and the other student got into a fight, and the principal tried to break it up. James punched the principal and continued to curse at him. Now he would be suspended.

Kelly now realized that her son was acting out because of her and his father's divorce. Now she must see the counselor for both her children's sake. Driving home, James didn't say a word. He just pouted with tears running down his face. Kelly figured she would give him time before she would find out what really happened at school. Kelly pulled up to the house. James got out and went straight to his room. Kelly sat down and picked up the phone. She called the counselor and made an appointment for her family. She also called the girls to help her move things into Kim's new apartment. They got together and moved and arranged Kim's things so when Kim and the baby came home, they would be comfortable. They also planned a baby shower for Kim when she returned home.

Vanessa sat up in her bed, not being able to sleep. She thought about all that had happened the last few months. She thought about the company going through its new change and her and Carl's promotions. Her feelings for Carl, should she give in to them or dismiss them? How she and Carl spent a lot of days and nights together.

She hadn't told anyone about a few kisses and close encounters that had taken place between the two of them, and she was curious to know how Carl was in bed. She thought about it a lot to herself. The next opportunity that presented itself she would take it. She thought to herself, *How would it look her f—— her boss?* She smiled and shook her head, saying to herself, *I have to think this through.*

She knew she wanted the job offer, but she also wanted more with Carl. Those late nights with him, would she be able to control herself, or would she even want to? She lay there and let her mind wander. What would she do? She would still have to work alone with this man.

Vanessa was putting the finishing pieces together to Kim's new home. Roberta and Jenny were getting things for tonight's baby shower. Kelly finished up with the kids at the family counselor, then left the kids to spend time with Dan, who was now back on his feet. Kelly headed to the hospital to pick up Kim and the baby to take them to their new home. Everyone was so happy they were coming home today when Kelly walked in, holding the baby in hand; and behind her, Kim walked in.

Kelly yelled, "Look who's home!"

Everyone ran to them, kissing and hugging. Jenny reached to hold the baby. "I am so happy to be home," said Kim.

KIM'S NEW HOME

She took off her coat, and Roberta undressed the baby. Vanessa handed Kim a cup of coffee. "Thank you!" said Kim, "but I could use a glass of wine, LOL."

Vanessa said, "Later."

Kim looked around the room. "This is very nice," she said.

Vanessa had found her a two-bedroom all on one level, no upstairs bedrooms. The bathroom was on the other side of the apartment, and her and the baby's bedrooms were next to each other. The kitchen and living room were very spacious. The ladies decorated everything the way Kim liked it, and they put baby bassinet in Kim's room for now, but they decorated the baby's room so nice.

Kim began to cry. She was so happy. She thanked them for all they had done for her and the baby. Jenny took the baby and laid her in the bassinet, and they all walked back to the living room, sat down, and began talking. They asked Kim how she felt.

"A little sore and tired," said Kim.

Vanessa suggested that they leave so Kim could get some rest and that they would be back later. Jenny said she would stay and if Kim needed anything she would be here. The others left, and Jenny took Kim to the bedroom to rest. Kelly went home to sleep awhile, being she had the house and the weekend to herself. Roberta was also on her own. The kids were with their father, and she went home and made her something to eat and watch TV. Jenny also went into Kim's living room and made phone calls to the caterer to confirm the time of the pickup for food, then checked on the baby and Kim. She sat down, had a glass of wine, and watched TV. As Vanessa entered her

BENT BUT NOT BROKEN

room, her phone rang. It was Carl. He had something he wanted to talk to Vanessa about. He asked if he could come over.

"Sure," said Vanessa. "Come on over."

REPOSITIONING

Carl would be coming over soon. Vanessa took a shower and put on a pot of coffee. As she had her first cup of coffee, the bell rang. It was Carl. Vanessa let him in and offered him a cup of coffee. She offered him a seat in the living room while she made it. Then she walked in, handed Carl a cup, and sat down beside him. She was nervous, and so was Carl. He kept fidgeting with his hands and had a very confused look on his face.

Vanessa asked, "So what is it you have on your mind?"

"You," said Carl. They both looked at each other and smiled. Carl said, "I mean have you decided on taking the job?"

Vanessa said, "Yes! I would be crazy not to!"

"Great," said Carl. "But there's something else on my mind." He looked at her and said, "I'm feeling you, and I can't seem to get you off my mind, and I wonder if you have the same feelings too. I mean if you don't, I understand."

Vanessa couldn't get the words out. She just grabbed him and kissed him, then it was on and popping. She couldn't believe she did that. And there it was, and they were in her bedroom. There was no paperwork being done that night. A lot of bodywork being done.

When all was done, Vanessa showered and began to prepare for the party, and Carl went home to do the same. After Carl got home and took a shower, he called Roberta.

"Hey, it's Carl. Do you have a minute to talk? I know you have to get ready for the baby shower, but I like to talk to you about the job offer. The board would like to know if you would consider the position in the PA office."

Roberta was happy that they considered her for the position. She asked, "When do you need the answer?"

He said, "ASAP, but we are not asking you to move there until after the trial, and you wouldn't have to worry about anything. The board is taking care of everything—travel, the house, any expenses. They just need your answer."

With great excitement, Roberta said yes.

"Well, we are all set," said Carl.

Roberta said yes and thank-you, and they hung up.

Kim woke up and looked around her. For a moment, she didn't recognize where she was, then Jenny walked in and said, "Hello, sleepy head, you're awake."

Kim said, "Girl, I almost didn't know where I was." They both laughed.

"Are you ready for tonight?" asked Jenny.

"Yes," said Kim and smiled.

"Okay, let's get you washed up while the baby is still asleep." She helped Kim get washed and dressed and helped with her hair and makeup, then sat her in the living room.

Kim looked around at all the baby decorations and smiled at Jenny. She said, "You are awesome!"

"I know," said Jenny and kissed Kim on the head. "Anything for you." Jenny went into the bedroom to get the baby dressed. After Jenny walked away, the bell rang. It was Roberta with the food. She gave Kim the baby, then opened the door. Roberta walked in carrying the food. She looked at Kim and smiled.

"Y'all look so cute," said Roberta and walked into the kitchen and set up the food. Then Jenny grabbed her keys and said she would be back after she got dressed. Roberta kissed Kim on the head and said, "Jenny tried to do your hair? You know white girls don't know nothing about black hair!"

"LOL, she tried," said Kim.

"Yes, she did," said Roberta. "Let me fix this mess."

Kim sat the baby in the sitter, and Roberta did her hair. The bell rang. It was Vanessa carrying a box of drinks. She asked Roberta to help her with the gifts out in the car. Roberta came back in with a few wrapped gifts while Vanessa brought in more gifts. Vanessa made Kim something to eat, then they had a drink and took a group picture before everyone came.

THE BABY SHOWER

They sat around laughing and talking. Vanessa said, "I finally did it, y'all!"

"Did what?" asked Roberta.

"Did Carl," said Vanessa. "And it was good!"

"OMG," said Roberta. They all laughed. Roberta told them she accepted the job offer and would be leaving after the trial. They all congratulated her. They would be sad when she would leave, but they were also happy for her. Now Kim would be Vanessa's number one on the job, but for now, she could work from home. And when she returned to work, they would help out with the baby until she found a sitter.

The bell rang. It was Carl. He carried a big gift box. He handed it to Kim and said, "Something for the baby." He greeted each lady, then Vanessa invited him to something to eat and drink. Kim and Vanessa smiled at each other as she led Carl off to the kitchen. Carl said to Vanessa, "I really enjoyed our time together."

Vanessa smiled and said, "So did I." They smiled at each other.

Then Carl said he looked forward to spending more time with her.

"I'd like that," said Vanessa. They kissed and walked into the room where everyone else was. The bell rang. It was Jenny. She came in with many gifts. Everyone complimented on how pretty she looked. She got herself a drink and turned on the music. She remembered not too loud because the baby was sleeping. They all felt little bad for Kim because her family couldn't be there. But they did find someone the baby would love to meet and they believed Kim needed to see. The women believed Kim would be able to handle this visitor. Jenny went into the bedroom to check the baby when the doorbell

65

rang, and people and gifts continued to come in and join the party. All of Kim's friends from work were there, and the gifts continued to stock up. As Jenny continued to change the baby, she heard the doorbell ring once again.

Restored

It was Mike bearing many gifts. Vanessa answered the bell, and when she saw Mike, she looked back at Kim, who had no idea what to do. She just stared back with a confused look on her face. Finally, she nodded to let him in.

Vanessa took the gifts from Mike and welcomed him in and offered him food and drink. He refused and walked over to Kim. He felt so bad seeing her in a wheelchair. He knelt down before her with tears in his eyes. All he could say was that he was very sorry. Everyone else decided to give them space to talk. Mike explained everything to Kim about their relationship and even his relationship with Nikki. He exposed that Nikki killed his wife and was blackmailing him to stay with her and that both of the children were not his, only the little girl. He said Nikki was never his wife; they never got married. He explained to Kim that he had custody of his daughter and wanted to be a part of her life.

Kim told him she had a baby. "Her name is Makayla. She is also your child."

Mike cried and said if Kim would give him another chance, he would do right by them both. He said he felt bad about Nikki's death, but now he could finally live a life he always dreamed of, and he would like her to be a part of that life as his wife. Kim didn't know what to say or do. She just needed time to think about all this. Mike asked if he could he see his baby.

Kim said, "Sure!" and Jenny came and wheeled her and Mike into the baby's room.

Jenny said, "I'll step out here, and if you need me, I'll be right here."

Mike asked, "Can I hold the baby?" Then he asked for her name again.

Kim said, "Makayla." They both smiled at her.

"She's beautiful," said Mike.

"Thanks!" said Kim. Tears continued to come down Mike's face. Kim had never seen this side of Mike, and she had to admit it was attractive, knowing how much she loved him. She loved him just a little bit more right at this moment. She thought to herself, *Mike's offer is just what I wanted, but I also must protect my heart and my baby's heart. I will have to pray about this.*

Mike said, "I'm not pushing, but please allow me to see her. You can see her, but as for me, it's going to take a few minutes to trust you again. You will have to earn my trust and love. I will, or I'll die trying." He kissed her forehead, and they joined the party. Everyone was having fun eating and drinking. And soon it was time to open the gifts. Vanessa made Kim a hat and sat her in the chair while she opened the gifts. Kim fought tooth and nail because she didn't want to wear the hat. She lost, and Kelly took a picture of all of them— mom, dad, and the baby. Everyone said, "How lovely they looked together."

Makayla got a lot of great gifts, and even her mom got a gift that night. Mike spent the night. Vanessa even got a party favor; Carl spent the night at her house. The welcome-home baby shower was such a big hit. Everyone enjoyed themselves. Reunions and love connections, it was all in all a great night.

The next day, Kim awoke to the smell of breakfast being made and being served in bed. Mike woke up early, fed, and changed the baby. Mike made Kim breakfast. Kim thought to herself, *I can get used to this,* as she smiled. The phone rang. It was Kelly calling to see how she could help with the baby, but Mike answered the phone and said, "I know it's your turn to help out with the baby, but I was wondering if I could do that for today. It would help me out a lot and help me to bond with Kim and the baby."

Kelly was pleased that he even wanted to help. She didn't care for Mike much, but she loved Kim, and Kim loved Mike. Kelly said she would call later and see how things were going. She decided to do some laundry and cleaning. Then the phone rang; it was Dan.

He wanted to know if he could come over and talk to her. When he came, he had papers in his hand. He told Kelly she would have to sign these papers. He explained what the papers were. It was a deed for the business. There were life insurance policies, and there was a will. He explained that he bought his partner out of the business, and Kelly would now be a partner. If anything was to happen to him, she would own the business free and clear. He was asking for nothing in the divorce except for visitation rights and his house and his car. He wanted her to put these papers in a safe place. He handed her the papers and keys to all the other properties. Kelly wondered what he was up to. She was glad he was being nice and all, but still he seemed weird. He said the doctor told him he could go back to work soon, but he wanted the weekend with the kids.

She agreed, and he then kissed her forehead and walked out the door. Vanessa and Carl had a good day planned. Lovely Sunday, Carl invited Vanessa to go to church with him. Vanessa enjoyed every moment of it. She met the pastor and was invited to go back to Carl's house for dinner later. Vanessa was spending the night with Carl tonight. It felt like a fairytale to Vanessa. She had never thought she could be this happy. Carl was everything she imagined he would be. She was feeling so blessed.

Roberta began to go through her closet and threw out the old things she no longer needed so she could make room for the new blessing now doing some spring cleaning. It was a good way for her to begin a new life. She thanked God for her new beginning.

OPEN BLIND EYES

The phone rang. It was Shirley telling Roberta she was coming over to talk, but Roberta forgot she had told Shirley she could come over. Roberta sounded confused. She hung up the phone and began to panic. She picked up the phone to call Vanessa but no answer. Then she thought to call Kelly, praying she would answer. The phone rang. Kelly said, "Hello!" The phone woke her up from her nap on the couch.

Roberta was yelling on the phone about Shirley coming over. She begged Kelly to come for the support. So Roberta made some coffee, hoping it would calm her down. Kelly would be there in a few minutes. She was on her second cup. When the doorbell rang, her heart skipped a beat. She thought it was Shirley, but when she opened the door, it was Kelly. Roberta hugged Kelly so tight.

Kelly said, "Please let me go and let me in." Roberta waved her into the house. Once they were inside, Kelly looked around, then went in the kitchen and saw the coffeepot on. She looked at Roberta and shook her head. She said, "We are going to need something much stronger than this!"

Roberta said, "Oh, I have something." She pulled out a bottle of Hennessy and made her and Kelly a drink. Kelly asked her if she was nervous. She handed Roberta a drink, then Kelly said, "Drink this straight. Have another, and you won't feel anything. We don't know what state of mind she is in."

A little while later, the bell rang again, and it was Shirley. By now, Roberta was feeling numb. When she opened the door, she welcomed Shirley in and asked if she could get her something to drink.

Shirley said, "Yes, please."

She introduced Shirley to Kelly and invited them to come inside the dining room to talk. Shirley started by saying she was sorry about what happened to Kim and wished her and the baby well. They both thanked Shirley, then she said, "I'm here to talk about my husband." Both girls looked at her, and she continued, "My husband is going away for life. My family is being broken apart. Trust me, he wasn't the best husband, but God knows I love him. And I know he has done a lot of bad things and is now being accused of some very vile things. I'm not saying that he hasn't done them, I'm just saying my heart has always belonged to him, and sometimes love can make you do some crazy things and even be blind to something."

"Yes, I know something about that," said Roberta. "My husband also had infidelities. With a man." Then she said, "I respect you, and I don't want to hurt you, but I need to tell you something about your husband. He raped me, and now I'm carrying his child."

Shirley's mouth dropped, and tears rolled down her face, putting her hands over her mouth. Kelly was also in tears. Shirley looked Roberta up and down and jumped up and punched Roberta. She ended with her hands around Roberta's neck. Kelly strained to pull Shirley's hands off Roberta's neck. When she finally got Shirley's hands away from Roberta, Shirley got up and walked away, crying out the door. They heard her drive off, screeching the wheels of her car.

Kelly put Roberta and her kids into her car and took them to spend the night at her house until she was sure Roberta would be safe. They called Kim and Vanessa and Jenny to let them know what occurred that night. Kelly explained that Shirley lunged at Roberta and punched her then choked her out but Kelly got her off Roberta and she ran away crying.

Vanessa asked, "Do you think she will come back?"

Kelly said, "I don't know, but I brought Roberta and the kids to my house." They all agreed that it was the safe thing to do. Kelly said, "We will all get up tomorrow at Kim's house." Kelly put Roberta back on the phone to assure them she was all right. When they were assured, they said good night.

After work the next day, they got together at Kim's house. The baby moved from hand to hand. Mike had gone to work. But Kim had given Mike permission to bring his other daughter over the house to be with her sister. The ladies got together. They prayed and discussed issues. They stayed by Kim's way into the evening. Before long, Mike came, and the ladies decided to leave. But they did get a chance to meet Mike's daughter, Shayla, who was excited to see her sister Makayla.

Jenny took the kids in to the room. Shayla fell in love with Makayla, and everyone could see it. Shayla spent the rest of the time with Makayla. Mike was so please his girls were getting along. As the night went down, Roberta said she was ready to go back to her own house. As she said this, her phone rang. It was Shirley saying she was sorry for her actions, and she wanted to apologize for what she did. She explained she was hurt and didn't know what to do but lash out. Shirley thanked Roberta for being honest with her and wanted to know if she could put her on speaker phone so she could apologize to the other women as well. They all accepted her apology. She stated that she felted crazy having to testify against her husband, and she was feeling some kind of way. She knew he was up to no good, but she hadn't gotten all the details together—lipstick on his clothing, the smell of perfume on his clothing. She said she knew he was up to no good, and she was sorry for all the hurt he caused them.

Shirley was sorry, and she began to cry. Roberta and the other women felt bad for her, and they invited her to lunch to meet with the other women she didn't know. Kim told Roberta to tell Shirley to meet them tomorrow at her house for lunch. All agreed, and all went their separate ways.

Trina, Jenny, Kim, Kelly, Vanessa, and Roberta sat down with Shirley for lunch, who said she knew something was going on when her husband stopped having sex with her. She said he would ask her to do things, and it always ended in him leaving her beaten, bloody, and sore. She would have done anything to please him, but she could never seemed to please him. When the abuse stopped, she was only happy he was no longer doing it to her. They hardly spoke unless he wanted to have sex and abuse her, then it appeared to Vanessa when

Roberta came in wearing the shades that Mr. Davis had given her the black eye and why Kim said what she said about Mr. Davis putting his hands on her again.

The women took time out to pray. Vanessa started by praying for Shirley. Kim prayed for Nikki. Shirley prayed for Roberta and her family. Kim and Jenny prayed for Vanessa and all families represented in the house. They also prayed over the food.

All sat down and ate and enjoyed one another's company. They were not allowed to discuss the case against Mr. Davis, but they discussed many other things that women talked about, like kids and relationships old and new. Without realizing it, these women had allow God in their lives, and he created a bond with these women that was not easily broken.

The morning of the trial, at the courthouse, they were all nervous, especially Kim. She would have to expose the secret she had been carrying so long. The firm's attorney met the women inside the courthouse as they all sat together, waiting. Jenny was called first. She told her story, and then Roberta and then Vanessa and then two other women, and last but not the least, there was Kim.

This trial went on for days, and the more days, the more intense the room was. The last day was Kim. The two women were called first and then Kim. She first began by letting the court know how she came to work for Mr. Davis, then she continued to talk about when things went wrong. She talked about working late with Mr. Davis one night and how he started making advances at her and how he backed her up against the wall. She tried to get away, but he pushed her down on the couch and told her if she didn't make love to him, she would lose her job and she wouldn't be able to work in any firm anywhere. He said that he had the power to destroy her, so if she told anyone, he would fire her. This went on a few times.

The first time, she found a bonus in her paycheck. Then he told her because she had an associate degree how he could make her partner in the farm. He had the power to sway the board to vote any way he wanted, and she had his vote. Kim said she stayed quiet for a while when she realized he had played her. She tried to deny him sex, and he beat her. He made sure they always worked alone. She didn't tell anyone because he told her no one would believe her and he would say she came on to him in order to move up in the company.

He said he would tell them that she was blackmailing him and the bonus in her paycheck would prove it. She didn't say anything for the sake of her career and reputation. Kim said she figured he had her because no one would hire her now. She worked hard for her associate degree and couldn't let him destroy everything she worked so hard for. Kim began to cry. She felt so ashamed. She had been holding on to this for so long. Again, she cried. Most of the court was in tears, including the judge. She looked up at the ladies and said, "I'm so sorry I didn't tell you all, but I didn't know how."

The judge told Kim she could step down. The girls embraced Kim, then they all sat down. Mike was there, and he held Kim in his arms and washed her eyes. She said it was all right. She was glad Mike was there. She also needed his encouragement. The court was told to go have lunch and return after.

THE DAVIES TRIAL

The woman returned back to the courtroom to hear the verdict. The verdict came back to find Mr. Davis guilty on all counts, sentenced to life. Shirley thought she would die on her own hearing this, but to her surprise, tears rolled down her face as she had very many mixed feelings about all that has been done. She made eye contact with her husband as they took him away in handcuffs. She ran out of the courtroom, crying.

Mr. Davis walked away with this confused look on his face, and each woman walked out with their own set of emotions as they walked out hand in hand as they departed each to their own homes. They decided to meet up later to celebrate. When Kelly returned home, she found Dan at the door, then Kelly with tears in her eyes just fell into Dan's arms and cried. Dan took her into the house and made her coffee while she sat on the couch, wiping her eyes. Dan handed Kelly a cup of coffee and said, "It's okay, it's over now."

Kim went home with Mike in tears and walked in the house straight to her bedroom and lay across the bed. Mike put the baby down and undressed her, changed her diaper, and made her a bottle. He gave Kim some space with her feelings. Roberta went home and had a shower and lay on the couch with her feelings, not sure what to do with them. Vanessa went home and into her room for deep prayer. Carl tried calling, but Vanessa just needed some time alone. Jenny went out for ice cream. Shirley went home and had a few drinks and cried. She felt so betrayed that night. No one really felt much like celebrating. Date night was cancelled. Each was alone with their feelings. Mike went into the bedroom to check in on Kim.

"Are you all right?" asked Mike.

"I'll live," said Kim. They both laughed. Kim sat up in the bed. Mike sat on the side of the bed. Kim said, "Thank you so much for being there today. You have done so much for me."

"Nowhere I'd rather be. Now can I lay down and hold you?" asked Mike.

"Yes, please," said Kim.

Dan came over and asked Kelly if she would mind if he stayed over. He wanted to be there for her.

"I don't mind. Thank you," said Kelly. She walked toward her bedroom and said, "I'm going to bed. See you in the morning." Kelly walked into the room and shut the door.

Vanessa called Carl back and asked him if he could come over. Carl said he would be right there. When he arrived, Vanessa hugged him so tight. Carl said, "It's all right. I'm here for you."

Roberta just lay on the couch until she fell asleep. Jenny went home and to bed. Shirley just passed out in the dining room. It was quite an emotional night for all. The next morning, Kelly had two homes to show. She got up early and showered and dressed, then she walked into the children's bedroom to see if they were up. She checked in each room, but the kids were not there. She walked downstairs to the kitchen only to find them already dressed and eating.

Dad had made breakfast, and he handed her a cup of coffee. Kelly smiled, remembering how he always made sure breakfast was served. The kids were ready for school. Dan smiled at Kelly and said, "Don't worry, I got the kids." He would take them to school so Kelly wouldn't be late for her appointment. She said thanks, and Dan and the kids walked toward the door. Then he looked back at her and said, "Can we have dinner tonight? I have something I would like to talk to you about."

"Sure!" said Kelly.

As Dan walked out the door, Kelly wondered what he could be up to. What did Dan want to talk about? That night, Dan took her to a restaurant they went to when they started dating. Dan and Kelly really enjoyed being at their old spot. After dinner, as they pulled up to the house, Kelly started to get out of the car. Just then, Dan stopped her and asked if he could continue the conversation in the house. They all entered the house. Kelly made coffee.

BACK TO REALITY

Kelly and Dan sat down for coffee, and the kids ran off to their rooms. Kelly asked Dan, "What is this all about?"

Dan said he had gone to the doctor and he had some bad news. Kelly had an awful feeling in the pit of her stomach. He continued, "I have cancer, K, and the doctor said it doesn't look good. She set up an appointment for me to get treatment right away at a treatment center a few miles from here. I'm leaving tonight. Lamar is driving me down. I wanted to talk to you first and ask that you just tell the kids I'm going away on business until I can tell them."

Kelly, with tears in her eyes, asked, "Is that why you gave me the papers?"

"Yes," said Dan, "with the HIV and now the cancer, my health is dangerously compromised. I don't know what will happen."

Kelly felt so bad for Dan and helpless, not a thing she could do to help. With tears in both of their eyes, they embraced each other. She thought how badly her family was falling apart and began to pray for her husband. As she looked in his eyes, she felt in her heart he would not be returning. Dan handed her a number.

"Here is all the info you will need." Kelly called the children down stairs to say good night to their father. The kids kissed and hugged Dan. Dan walked out the door. He and Lamar were heading to check in to the treatment center. Lamar would stay in a hotel while Dan did his treatment, but they would spend the rest of the time together. Lamar would soon find a place to live near the hospital so he could be close to Dan.

Carl and Vanessa living the fairy-tale life. They seemed to fit together like a perfect pair of gloves, spending every waking hour together day and night. At work, it was all business. At church, it was all about Jesus. At home, it was all about them. They took turns spending the night at each other, house and cooking, at times deciding where they would go and what they would do.

Vanessa now made friends at church, including the first lady. She became very active in church. The first lady had Vanessa running the Women's Ministry and implemented her women's group within the church. The first lady also attended meetings, as well as the women of the church and women of the community. The group had now reached a wide range of women. More families were joining the church, getting baptized. The community was more unified than ever. God's love and unity created a bond not easily broken. Families were being restored. Marriages were mended. Healing was taking place for the broken, and now the blind was seeing for the first time in their lives. The lame was walking upright.

Carl proposed to Vanessa in church one Sunday. She said yes. Now, they are engaged and moved in together. Kim and Mike had joined the church with their new family of four. Makayla now has her big sister Shayla, and the family would be baptized together. Mike had now found a job working for Dan at the construction yard, and he also shared his story as a motivational speaker. Kim was now working with Vanessa and was now writing a book telling her story—*Had It Not Been for God's Grace and Mercy, She Wouldn't Have Made It.*

Roberta and her children moved down to PA and are loving it. Roberta and her children loved their new home and schools. Her son Paul would be attending graduation and going on to college on a full scholarship in playing pro basketball. Roberta and her children were still seeing a counselor and had made a lot of progress. Roberta's daughter Kate had now joined the cheerleading squad in high school. She had made many friends and come out of her shyness and now popular. Roberta loved her new job and her new home. She attended a new church faithfully every Sunday. She was now a missionary.

Saturdays she went out and spoke with teenage girls to share her experiences about God and Women of Encouragement, who saved her life and gave her a hope and a new family and sisters she genuinely loved. She knew they genuinely love her.

Roberta was even dating now. She loved and was amazed that God had opened her eyes and allowed her to see her children happy and growing into beautiful adults. Also, she saw these other teen girls that God placed in her life spouting into lovely flowers. She and Lamar were co-parenting, and they even had a friendship now. No, they didn't hang out, but they do speak and respect each other. Lamar had found a house where he and Dan lived, and they all pretty much respected each other's space and time with the children.

Dan was still receiving treatment and was making the best of it. He had accepted his fate and had his relationship with God and had asked God's forgiveness. He believed he had received it.

I'd like to tell you Dan and Lamar attended church, but I wouldn't, because they didn't. They lived a quiet life together, and they enjoyed their time with their children when they had them. They both tried to set their weekend with the kids at the same time, and they went out and did family fun things. They shopped and ate together. They went to fun places and movies. They also planned things for the kids to do. They took family vacation. They kids enjoyed spending time with their fathers. There was no judgment there. The most favored vacation was Disney World. Vanessa and Roberta met them down there, and they had so much fun! The kids would always say it was the best vacation ever. As Lamar and Dan looked through their picture book, they realized how much the children had grown, and to them, it seemed so fast. But they soon realized how blessed they were to be able to see the transformation, and they said, "To God be the glory."

Shirley's mom fell sick, and she moved back home to take care of her. She was happy to be back home and able to be there for her mom. She started her real-estate business down there. She was enjoying being able to live her dream of being the owner of her business. She had found counseling for herself and still dealing with some old hurts and emotions, but all in all, she was happy. She had even met up with some of her old friends she was raised with. They do a lot of things together, going out and such. She met an old-time crush. She was not ready to date yet, but was working on that too.

A few months of her being back home, she lost her mom. The women all went down to comfort her. They stayed with her until she was able to be back on her feet. She was so surprised to see they all showed up, but like what they told her, theirs was a bond not easily broken, and they were sisters for life. There was nowhere they would rather be than with her at a time like this. They stuck together through all kinds of weather. This was what Women of Encouragement was all about—sisters helping each other.

They all still kept in touch no matter where they were. They talked on the phones every day. They stuck like glue. Shirley had been very successful in her business. She had grown in her walk of life. She still got letter from Mr. Davis. Although she got everything after the divorce, she was over him and did not respond to him. Shirley was now living her life to the fullest.

Jenny joined the church and had made new friends. She now had a new boyfriend name Rob, whom she met at church. They were now spending all their time together. She had been promoted at work and now had her own office. Now Jenny was loving her life. She brought a new car and remodeled her home. She also now had custody of her sister's daughter, who was eight. She was very happy with her family life. She still kept a close eye on Kim and the kids.

She really admired Kim. Jenny had been so beaten down by life and love. Her last relationship was abusive for years with this guy name Chuck. He would beat her and call her every name under the sun. His oral abuse stuck in her so deep she wore it like a garment. He had her self-esteem so beaten down that she believed that she was not worthy and her words didn't mean anything to anyone. It was best she kept her mouth closed. She was so glad to be free of him. When he was arrested for robbery, she got her things together and jumped on the first thing, smoking, to get away from him. She ended up in New York and began bringing the pieces of her life together. She had to do some things she was not proud of, but now as she looked back over her life, she thanked God for his grace and mercy, for all he had done for her.

She was now living the life she always wished she would with the help of God and the women in her life. She felt it was all worth it, being with people who really loved her. She had a good job, home, and family who loved her. She was finally finding what it felt like to be in love. Jenny and Rob had been spending a lot of time with each other and had fallen in love with each other. He was so good with her niece, and they had so much fun together. It had gotten her thinking about a family of her own with Rob. The women seemed to like Rob and the fact that Jenny had found someone to love.

God has a way of making a way out of no way, for he knows the plans he has for us through prayer and supplication. Letting our request be known on to God and not leaning on our own understanding. Walking by faith and not by sight. Being obedient to the spirit of God. Believing he will bring us through and restore our life to the life he intended. However, being disobedient can lead us into a life of confusion and lead us off-track or out of alignment to his will.

Kim had to learn the lesson of being disobedient and learning to wait on God, but because she went ahead of God's timing, she moved out of his path and had to be put back in place. Until she would surrender, God would work it out. Sometimes, we humans want what we want and move in the wrong way to get it. Sometime we think God is saying no to what we want. Most of the time, he says, "In my timing, not yours." God needs to go before us and make the crooked place straight. And when we don't obey, we have to pay the price. But God will work it out according to his will and give you more than you could ask or think.

Mike has learned that when God blesses you and you take it for granted, he will remove it, allowing you to know what it is to loss something so special to God and man. He will allow you to miss the various things you took for granted.

Mr. Davis has learned the lesson of reaping what you sow. You can't treat people any way you want because you feel you have power over them. The deeds you put out shall return back to you.

Kelly has realized that you can't put anything or anybody on God's throne, because God is the only one fit to sit on the throne, and God should be the only one you want to sit on the throne in your life. Anything or anyone else will crumble and fall; God is the only one who is able to mend it back together and restore all that was lost.

Jenny has realized that God is an awesome God and that if you open your heart to God, he will come into your life and give you beauty for ashes. God heals and restores all the broken pieces of your life, and he builds you up to become a wonderfully made woman.

Vanessa has learned that leaning and depending on God is the best place to be in life. You must open your heart to love, compassion, and unity; and God will multiply the seed and produce a wonderful garden of beautiful flowers that are called people. To God be the glory to all.

Roberta has learned that to stand firm on God's Word would build a strong foundation that would bring her through anything. Holding on to God's unchanging hands, they all have learned that it is important to stay in touch with God every day and to walk in God's love, putting faith in God first no matter what. It would please God and keep you focused when walking with him. God is the same today, yesterday, and forever. He is love and wants you to share that love with someone who doesn't know him and how much he loves them. Walking in God's love daily is the greatest gift of all. Acknowledge God in all things. May his praise be in our mouths always.

About the Author

Jacquline Dawson, a forty-nine year old African American woman, was born in Passaic, New Jersey. Single mom of three adult children, and grandmother of five. She lived outside of Passaic for most of her life. She now resides in Clifton, New Jersey. She received her credentials in psychology and social work from Stratford University of Vermont. The founder of both non-profit organizations, Women Of Encouragement Inc. and Change Generation youth center, which began in the comfort of her own home. She brings women and youth together so that they may have a safe and secure environment where they can find love and non-judgement to work through the hardships of life and find positive solutions in peace and love.

CPSIA information can be obtained
at www.ICGtesting.com
Printed in the USA
LVHW110807191119
637819LV00009B/1154/P